WE HAVE BEEN LUCKY
IN THE MIDST OF MISFORTUNE

WE HAVE BEEN LUCKY
IN THE MIDST OF MISFORTUNE

Poems by

Sarah Stern

Kelsay Books

Cover photograph provided by the Rexingen, Germany Archives

Cover design by Shay Culligan

Author photograph by Claire Holt~
www.claireholtphotography.com

ISBN: 978-1-949229-40-0

Kelsay Books
Aldrich Press
www.kelsaybooks.com

Praise for Sarah Stern

"Sarah Stern has written an utterly frank, headlong, passionate, and deeply engendered book of a woman in mid-life. She writes out of her own longings, her devotions as a daughter and a mother, her fiery supplications. *But Today is Different* may be printed with ink, but it was written with fire."

—Edward Hirsch, author of *A Poet's Glossary* and *The Living Fire, New and Selected Poems*

"Sarah Stern's first collection of poems, *But Today Is Different*, is a marvel. Wise, compassionate, erotic, plain-spoken, studded with wonderful moments—a black goat with blue eyes, an aging mother's clavicle 'like a Calder mobile,' an iconic lipstick stain on a coffee cup—Stern's vision puts a shine on the ordinary (a trip to Macy's, a scraped knee) and gives it back to us as something wondrous and new. A new voice, in which readers will hear echoes of Philip Levine and Grace Paley...and a real achievement."

—Cynthia Zarin, author of *The Ada Poems* and *An Enlarged Heart: A Personal History*

"In *Another Word for Love,* Sarah Stern searches for meaning in a broken world. She delights in things around her, whether the El in New York or trees in New Hampshire, finding in them keys to her inner life. I read this book in the light of her clarity, exactitude, and fine intelligence."

—Grace Schulman, author of *Without A Claim*

"Vivid and opaque, innocent and sophisticated, Sarah Stern's poems in *Another Word for Love* are so full of life, never more than when they hint at death, that they refuse to sit still on the page. It's us she's catching in these glimmering nets."

—Karen Durbin, *Elle*

"Sarah Stern is a poet to watch and relish."

—*Jewish Book World*

For Willie and Zoe
And, as always,
for Michael

Acknowledgments

Grateful acknowledgement to the following publications in which these poems, some in earlier versions, first appeared.

Autumn Sky Poetry: "Talkeetna, Alaska"
Bayou: "Fragment" and "Antibes in Spring"
Coffee Poems Anthology: "The Interview"
Curious Rooms: "Keeping Busy"
Ducts.org: "Fireworks at Wilmington"
Epiphany: "At the Market," "Feeding the Elephants," and "*Pura Vida* in Costa Rica"
First Literary Review-East: "At 42" and "Father Turns 80"
FreeFall: "Wait, One More Dream"
The Mid-America Poetry Review: "Sunnies"
The New Verse News: "To:" and "Protest at Union Square, November 12, 2016"
Parting Gifts: "Making Jam"
Poetica Magazine: "Father Reads Noah's Story from the Torah"
Rise Up Review: "Swimming in the Trump Years"
Seedhouse: "Separate Seating" and "The Tracks"
Swwim: "A Night Thought Can't Sleep"
This Full Green Hour: An Anthology by the One O'Clock Poets: "Mercury"
Treasure House: "Her Boutique" and "The Soft Spot"
Verse Daily: "*Pura Vida* in Costa Rica"
Women Writers in Bloom Poetry Salon: "Three Daughters"
What Rough Beast, Indolent Books: "Moss" and "Haigerloch Sisters"
The Woven Tale Press: Arts and Literary Journal: "Slow Dance," "Bending Toward Justice," "Horsewoman and Camels," and "Nasturtiums"

With much appreciation and affection for the One O'clock Poets (additional appreciation for John Couturier's proofreading and editing) and the Bronx Best Poets. With love to family and friends who have encouraged me all these years. With special thanks to Marilyn Kallet, Brooks Haxton, Yerra Sugarman, Edward Hirsch, Cynthia Zarin, Grace Schulman, Andrew Nagorski, Karen Durbin, and the Bronx Council on the Arts. With further appreciation for Kelsay Books, especially for Karen Kelsay.

With immeasurable love and gratitude to my husband, Michael, and children, Willie and Zoe.

Contents

Part III: Keeping Busy

Part IV: Now She's in the World

Part V: The Little Room

Part VI: What I Was Then

Part I:

Your Private Moments

Guadeloupe

One winter we camped in Guadeloupe.
Mom and Dad, all my brothers, and then sister-in-law.

Dad wrapped his head in a wet, white t-shirt—a makeshift turban.
Yul Brynner bald he was, but it took me years to notice.

Mom's holding my hands up over my head next to the warm ocean.
It was the early '70s. One of the few times we were all together.

Our tent was army green. We hiked up to the volcano.
Banana leaves. A machete in the mist.

There's a grainy movie somewhere in the old house,
how we remember our parents' voices.

They believed in us, but what do parents know.
We are of them and all that luck. Luck.

We roasted strange fish on the fire,
got a rash from those oozing plants. Sunburnt too.

In the picture, I have no top on, short hair, smiling.
The air was salty and the sugar buds were years away.

At the Bronx Zoo

Gorilla mom brings
baby close to the window
To show us now—*Look.*

Cradles in her arm,
As mine were too, she stares
at me. *Who are you*?

Before I could say,
she pulls her close, leaving me
with this thought: *Find out.*

Emptying the Dishwasher

He does the cups
I do the plates
He does the glasses
Then we take turns
With the knives and forks
And spoons

He's standing there smiling
Done we say for now
As the coffee brews
In the office kitchen
Small delicious talk
As we wait
For the green *Ready*
To flash on the industrial maker

We get our cups
The brand's funny bitter we say
Adding milk and sugar
I'm already thinking
About the poem I will write

He does the cups
I do the plates
He does the glasses
Then we take turns
With the knives and forks
And spoons.

First Frost Night

You let me go, sweet grief,
first and always love,
you will be with me

as long as I want you.
It was you.
You came back one more time,

hummingbird, greenblack mouse,
hovering in the week
after your death.

When I look in the mirror
and I see your mouth
I want you to say something.

Leaves turning in the sea sway
on a weekday morning.
I want you to see them.

I want to fall back with you
and fall back again
at 2:00 a.m.

There you are—
on a first frost night
my age now.

Horsewoman and Camels

She kept smiling at me
but looking about me too
as if I were the center of a framed collage:

There were camels in a row, cupcakes,
night lamps, a pigeon, perfume bottles,
a bicycle, a drill, a four-post bed, one shoe,
her bras hanging on the line, lots of shadow.

I wanted to know what was making her so happy.
I asked and she shouted back at me from across the river.
I couldn't hear a sound
but I saw her mouth—*You*.

I woke up in the dark light,
the wheels of things spinning wet sparks,
horsewoman and camel, sweet mommy.
How she left me upright.

Bending Toward Justice

There are more than four seasons,
I hear someone behind me say
in the large jury room
before we're asked to pay attention

and remember our numbers. King's
The arc of the moral universe…
hangs from the ceiling
reminding me of the Passover death angel

swallowed in flames.
The bus ride here—
a parade of small wonders—
Christmas approaching

the strollers and mothers
the high schoolers, cascading about
as we all move down
the Grand Concourse.

I was once lonely in San Francisco
and my mother said
just take a bus
across the city.

See what you can see.
How she enjoyed the ride.
And now, the string of lights are
blowing wildly over the boulevard

as if there is a fifth season
somewhere out there
in the half dome
of a Bronx afternoon.

My Little Life

My little life, the thought of it
All of us here and now have one
Our loves, what makes us happy, what turns us on
What grows in our garden

Mother would say as long as there is something on the table to eat
Yes, that's true, but
After we have that, we get to look around at who is sitting with us
Let us praise them and the light too.

Nasturtiums

I eat its red flower
this afternoon spread
on toast with cheese,
thinking of you in this light.

    And you far off—
    another country
    another woman
    another life.

I eat another one
without you.
A strange muscle-beast you are: tongue—
crucial for taste and articulation

    for what could have been, too—
    the two of us
    two tongues, two flowers.
    Two nothings now.

Glimpses

She said *let it go*
    So I did.
        Like an orange balloon on a string

It kept rising higher and higher
    Over the trees
        Until I couldn't see it anymore

But that's not what happens with you
    You rise and float and return to me
        As though I never let you go

Please, let me be
    As I'm learning to live
        Without you

Every now and again
    I get glimpses
        Of what that would look like

The orange of you out there
    Disappearing behind the rooftops
        Absence has its own color.

I'm not good at letting go.
    She said—
        You don't have to be.

Talkeetna, Alaska

Salmonberry scat piles
In the middle of the trail

Mountain goats, moose on permafrost
Fireweed ice cream in town

Otter eating crabs—sleek pashas of the harbor
Glaciers calving, blue thunder

Seals sleeping on the narrow
Paying us no mind

In the Pacific
We are temporary

The orcas—a matriarchy—
The biggest momma's boys around

The captain of our one-day cruise tells us
Her sons stay with her their whole lives

At the roadhouse with the bathroom
Down the hall, I couldn't sleep

I keep thinking of her like that—arched in midair
Her white markings ablaze.

Pool Visits

Swimming in the pool last night, I was thinking about how the dead stay with us through their guest appearances. Father comes to me often in the water and makes me laugh at something and then I get water in my nose. Mother, too, but when she appears I cry, making my goggles fog up. It's often about what I wanted her to know, and what she'd say. And then they're gone.

Slow Dance

When evil appears dead center
I turn to the trees
and ask them what's next.

They answer bit by bit,
their leaves about them like pupils,
branches undulating in the breeze.

What next?
Shadows across their gray
trunks, blue skies,

clouds, mercy visible.
There will always be mothers
telling their children

to stay in school
to look at the white cat
to eat a good lunch.

We are a vile species—
murder, rape and desecration.
The trees know it—

in their wayward rustling,
their purposeful posture,
their slow dance toward winter.

The Yellow Lines

Freshly painted and symmetrical
Rising slightly off the pavement

They make me think of what could be done
While I'm still here, winter gone

Bougainvillea blooming in the Bronx,
While I can remember it was you—

Yellow dividing the road
Look, the white cat crosses for the first time

No cars, too early
Just she and I and the lines

That mark the block and beyond
In this willow-wide summer

Smell the skunk too
Far away now, what bravado

To leave your scent like that
You've done it with me, through me

Down my belly
Who said we run in parallel

With someone we will never meet
But in a dreamscape—

Yellow skunk demon, catbird
Paint me too.

To:

Boil seven brown eggs in water
Turn off the kitchen light as the day begins
See the sparrows perched, earrings, on winter trees
Miss you—all of you—always
See the banner headlines and hope still
Know that we are here now
Forget not what makes us happy
Pee clear with no pain
Love you forever, even when I'm gone.

Protest at Union Square, November 12, 2016

This is what democracy looks like
      Radishes, scallions, and brown bread
No hate, no fear, immigrants are welcome here
      Emma Lazarus, let's please have lunch today

Give me your tired, your poor, your huddled masses
      You wrote that poem already
A prayer for our country
      Emma Lazarus, come with me to shul today

Sit with me under Lady Liberty
      The New York Harbor, Leonard Cohen, *Hallelujah*
The little girl on her dad's shoulders down 16th Street
      Holding on with me.

Swimming in the Trump Years

Yes, even under water you manage
To accompany me, but I'm working on it.
I bought a new suit, crossed back,
for racing competitions, the catalog exclaims.

The thoughts still float—
The woman from Botswana I met last night
Told me that her mother had 17 types of fruit trees back home
And did I know that beetles are a good source of protein.

I did not.
I don't know much. I like to say that out loud sometimes.
I don't know anything, really.
What do we know?

Mom loved the word "limitations."
She'd say we all have limitations.
Yes, we do.
It's freeing to think about that, our limitations.

I went for my yearly checkup.
My doctor in Yonkers felt my ovaries
And said that they are growing smaller.
I want to hold and cuddle them.

I imagine them to be robin-egg blue
Tiffany's. Oh no. Stop.
My beautiful small ovaries—
Stay with me a little more.

I needed a quarter for the meter,
But only had two dimes and a nickel.
Asked the UPS man, yes, and he wouldn't take my change.
"I got plenty in the truck."

Sometimes a sentence
Makes you love a stranger.
Just like that.
You're grateful

For a few words and your
American dream, your chlorine,
Your private moments
of pure exaltation.

Part II:

We Have Been Lucky in the Midst of Misfortune

With and Without Hats, A Charted History

Barbara begins with two photographs:
my grandfather Julius and his 9 siblings
Isaak
Sigmund
Max
Abraham
Fanny
Friedericke
Rosa
Jette
Augusta

The five brothers standing behind their sisters, who are sitting, but you can't see chairs. In the first, the men have hats, the second they don't. Minuscule shifts in expression between them. Look, Fanny is smiling slightly in the second and Isaak squinting more (handsome in a bowtie, strong nose, broad shoulders, deported to Riga, November 28, 1941). "Isaak didn't make it out." My great uncle. Mother told me things selectively.

Their parents Elias and Sophie had 13 children. Two died in infancy—Leopold (1869-1870) and Anonymous (1872-1872).

And then there was Hannchen who "ran off with the Gentile shepherd (Karl Rummele 1856-1908) and they sat shiva for her." (Mother never told me this.)

Barbara shows me a third photo of Hannchen with Karl and their 3 children. "Sigmund's son Alfred would visit her on the sly and bring her money."

All their names in a chart:
Personen-Datenblatt für Geschwister Pressburger.

Under Julius, born March 25, 1884
verheiratet mit Klara Schweizer (my grandmother)
Eltern von Helene Gribetz (my mother once had an *e* on her name).
Give it back to me
und Sigrete (my aunt Gretel)
1939 flieht die Familie in die USA

in die USA I am
I understand *mutter, vater, geboren, gestorben.*

Mother, father, born, died.
We're eating pretzels and the coffee is good with
Barbara and Heinz in Horb,
the Neckar River curves through the town
like mother described, there are swans too.

Two Letters

Inadequate,
This small boat riding toward you will not make it.
Sit with me. I give you your story.
You were born on March 25, 1884.
You died on November 9, 1953.

*

You were awarded the Iron Cross II Class with Wurttemberg and Bavarian Silver Military Medals of Honor in World War I.

Twenty years after your service, on November 9, 1938, Kristallnacht / Pogromnacht, you were arrested with 10 others, and then sent to Dachau for four weeks, a work camp then. Released, you were able to escape to New York in August 1939 with your wife and daughter, my mother. Gretel already in New York.

Mother loved the fat cockroaches and the smell of hot dogs from the cart. She wanted desperately to lose her accent. She did.

You worked at the Loews Movie Theater cleaning toilets. You bought a small house in Monroe, Connecticut, near your cousin Heddy and her husband Viggy.

I have two letters you wrote from the front lines
to Mayor Kinkele of Rexingen.

*

December 4, 1914

Dear Mayor Kinkele,

I was delighted to receive your much appreciated letter with the enclosure. Many thanks! I was particularly pleased to hear that you and your dear family are all keeping well as I am, thank God! Since I left home I have gone through a lot and have had to witness so much horror.

I would never have believed that human beings could be so cruel to each other. I am a corporal in the cavalry with the baggage convoy. My men and I haven't got out of our boots or clothes for the whole 12 weeks since the war began. Nor have we slept under a roof up to now. We always have to march by night and at the very start we were attacked in Alsace by francs-tireurs, French soldiers.

Thank God we got off fairly lightly and only lost 4 men and 16 horses. From Alsace we proceeded to the area around Reims where things were better than in Alsace and now we are in Flanders. I'm in charge of 12 drivers and 24 horses which is no easy matter, given the rough undeveloped ground, and often by night I have to go ahead with reinforcements while the bullets and shrapnel whiz around my head!

It's a horrible sight, going through burning villages, passing over masses of dead bodies. But in spite of the toil and deprivation, we are willingly in battle, conscious that we are keeping the war away from our country, fighting for King and Fatherland.

The people here in whose country war is raging are really in a dreadful state. Their horses, cattle, hay and straw confiscated, they are left with nothing but their bare lives, and that in the middle of winter, so that we sometimes have to give them food.

I have shared many a piece of bread with the poorest of them.

But enough for today! With every good wish to you and your dear family. Merry Christmas!

Yours,
Corporal Pressburger
Auf Wiedersehen.

*

January 27, 1915

Dear Mayor Kinkele,

I received your letter which means so much to me. I'm glad to hear that you and your dear family are in good health as I am so far, God be praised!

Thanks, too, for what you sent. I have survived many dangerous situations lately, thanks be to God! At night I often have to go back and forth with wagon-loads of straw and food and bring arms and equipment right up to the firing line, where I have often been caught up in shell fire.

Just recently, as I advanced somewhat carelessly by daylight, an English aircraft spotted us and immediately we were struck by about 10 shells in front of, beside and behind us. But the greatest misfortune was that – at just that moment – we overturned a fully-loaded wagon! And yet, over and over again, we have been lucky in the midst of misfortune.

With best wishes, dear Mayor Kinkele, to you and the whole family.

Yours,
Corporal Pressburger

*

We are keeping the war away from our country,
fighting for King and Fatherland.

I have shared many a piece of bread with the poorest of them.

Merry Christmas.

And yet, over and over again,
we have been lucky in the midst of misfortune.

*

Mother loved you so.
From time to time out of nowhere,
as if a wave of you rode over her,
she'd speak of you.

Moss

Elias Wolf Pressburger
Sophie Pressburger
My great grandparents.
Heinz and Barbara take us up the hill
To the Jewish cemetery
It's raining
Barbara says, "The graveyard is beautiful in every season."

The stones take us further and further back
The 1600s
The all-shades-of-green moss
Cover everything
We are under water
In a land of gorgeous fish and names
A black chill rises and thick vines roar
Write my name here.

> I could have been a middle-aged woman in Berlin.
> Boots and jeans, kinky just right. *Glühwein.*
> I cry for the numbers.
> Fish have no end—see them in this small green.

Is this what it means—to see the past in front of you?
Even the still-visible smashed glass is lyrical
Even in death you try to take from us
But you can't
We are on the other side already
Ha—bastards.

Mommy, I feel you here
I'm remembering how you told me you'd play,
Run and hear the church bells
I see the village below, the pastel houses
Fields, the fields you spoke of
How your papa would come home from

A week of cattle dealing
And he'd ask you—

"Who did you beat up this week?"
Because you were strong
And he loved you.

Bergstrasse 41, Rexingen 2015

My mother's house.
Now Turks live here, a photo
of me now by the front door, calico, too. Here kitty.

Above the Stars

The Nazis made the Jews record everything
they took with them. Heinz pointed out that
the Jewish farmers had many books, yes, Schiller, too:

> *World, do you know your creator?*
> *Seek him in the heavens;*
> *Above the stars must He dwell.*

The Church Bells

We heard them today
in the cemetery
Mommy, you listened to them on your back
in the tall grass up on this hill.
It was so peaceful, you said.

Cemetery in Basingen (town neighboring Rexingen)

The cemetery.
So many Cohanim hands
on the tombstones.
My Oma Klara was born in Basingen on May 3, 1889.

I spent summers in Monroe, Connecticut.
When I didn't have day camp,
we went to visit Susan and Inga, sisters,
who lived in Bridgeport.
We'd go to the beach together.
Susan and Inga were from Basingen.
Susan worked at Alexander's
in the Trumbull Shopping Center.
She smoked, had a deep raspy voice.
Inga was funny.
They both wore fancy bathing suits.
I liked them very much.

Haigerloch Sisters

We'd visit Selma and Berta on their Catskills farm every summer.
Mom always said, *We're going to Haigerloch.*
All these years I thought she made the name up,
but it was another town in the *Schwarzwald.*
I have a photo of its big yellow sign.

Selma and Berta were from Haigerloch.
Berta's long gray braids
crowned her head.
Her smile spanned farther than her teeth.

Selma was the quiet sister.
Their house sat crookedly opposite the barn.
The dining room had a heavy
German table, a picture of her husband

and son with Selma's eyes.
Both shot July 1941 in Theresienstadt.
Berta and Selma must have
had 20 dogs, more cats.

Chicken eggs all over.
Selma milked the cows,
pulling at them efficiently
as she sat on a stool.

We'd pitch a tent on a hilltop, as far
as the station wagon could go.
Make a fire.
Fry eggs in the morning.

The cows were named stars there—
Johnny Carson was an ornery bull.
I remember so much cow shit
and the dogs, yelping, wild in the valley.

Berta fed the calves.
She let me feel their sandpaper
tongues. My whole hand
in their mouths.

Cafe Levi

Before the war there was a cafe in Horb,
down the hill from Rexingen.
You could sit and talk there.

For Barbara and Heinz

Barbara and Heinz drive us
to the airport.
In the car, we talk
mommy's Schwäbisch:

Guck a mole—look here
Zwetschekuche—plum cake
Kartoffelsalat—potato salad
Du bisch so dick—you are too fat.

Mommy's so close I can feel her.
We've arrived and Barbara
follows the Departure signs
until we are by the curb.

We open the trunk,
pull the suitcases out.
All of us overcome in this
December Stuttgart morning—

to almost love, somehow,
to say that we were here, now.
Mommy, you never really left.
But you did.

You had many lives.
I want you to come back
so we can talk about them.
Now that I've seen the house and the Neckar swans,

tell me who else you loved—
who you really were.
We roll our bags through the revolving door,
Barbara and Heinz drive back to Horb.

Making Love in Berlin

Yes, we did, late night
the Christmas markets not far
Einstein Kaffee near.

Part III:

Keeping Busy

On Audubon Avenue

She said the pain
ran up her nose,
behind her eyes
until the blood thinners
made their way.

That moment you bring
a straw to your mother's mouth,
you're no longer the child.
In the green room
with the monitors,
the beautiful patterns
the heart makes.

When she was young
the Irish bus driver
waited for her
on Audubon Avenue, en route
to her Local 65 job.
She'd run, red hair and freckles,
letting go, turning into an American.

Mercury

I dreamt of fish.
They were small and I was letting them go,
pouring a bag into the pond.

Summer.
That slowness coming up
out of the sidewalk grass.

Jonas catches a dragonfly,
green legs and wings,
Mercury has no moon.

Cherries after my Aunt Gretel's funeral.
Juice runs down my chin.
My fingers are stained

red like meat my aunt
would hang in her butcher shop
on Columbus Avenue in 1972.

If someone stole a chicken
she ran after them.
And said, "If you really need it, take it.

But don't take without asking."
Gretel would tell this often,
gesturing with her large hands.

Keeping Busy

Now that Death has looked at me
I walk along the water's edge,
showing her my house of willow trees.

Everyone is busy. So am I.
I walk along the water's edge.
Now that Death has looked at me

I show her my house of willow trees,
the baseball game beyond the hedge.
Everyone is busy. So am I.

Now that death has looked at me
I think of her in the blue light.
The batter cracks the wind in two.

I walk along the water's edge,
show her my house of willow trees.
The sun goes down far and wide.

A Night Thought Can't Sleep

It stands up and
takes you on the bus.

Blue jay feather in grass—
summer in City Island.

The drawbridge.
Fishing off the side

and the kids running back
and forth. *What d'yah catch?*

Orchard Beach
two women dance

on Saturday afternoon.
Tattooed boys look on.

Mother says *keep
writing. It's what you have.*

Give me the words that
grind us into meaning like

those two on the plaza:
forgiveness and wild gesture.

He was talking in that way

that made you think
you could speak with him for hours.
The way he paused just before

answering; he was thinking
about a good answer, words mattered.
Good question, he said.

You spoke for an hour,
you knew nothing about him,
just the way he paused before speaking.

He was married once.
You were caught in the pause—
the spot below his nose

above his lips, unclaimed territory.
You stopped there and traced
that space with your fingertip

until all that was left
was a question mark.
How far would you go

that October afternoon,
before the leaves changed,
the way he opened the door

for you and you caught him
looking at you.
You could stay awhile and talk

have coffee together
until the moon rose
over Amsterdam Avenue.

The Interview

Tell me about the time
before you knew it all,
when you were just starting out
buying the things you needed.

Peel away the layers
of what you want me to think
and just talk.
Talk about the shoes,

the light-colored sweater,
the roses, the small roses you
said spilled over the fence.
Tell me about the first kiss,

the way it felt.
You knew from then on
that kisses stopped things
like STOP signs, because if I remember, you said

that's when you knew that
life wasn't going to be a series of
forwards, instead more
backwards than forwards.

At the end of your life
if you're lucky you'll be
right where you started, in the beginning,
with the sun and water.

Tell me about the coffee
with your mother and father
before school and the square of sugar.
Speak slowly.

Yours, Heng

Every third day
Heng-Fu and I
worked in the Berkeley
co-op kitchen. At first, he
didn't talk to me.

When I would say,
"Hi. How are you?"
He would nod and look away.
One day, he told me
he was from Cambodia.

Then I told him about my mother.
We spoke of the Black Forest,
rice fields, America.
His face was still
like pond water.

We still write
letters to each
other. "Yours, Heng"
he ends in his small
wing-like writing.

Wait, One More Dream

Nobody really knows what's going on.

¾ cup of flour, ¼ cup of whisper

Dark matter teases and obsesses astronomers.

Invisible "missing mass" requires gravitational
glue to hold clusters of galaxies together.

So it was love all along

The sky could be a different story.

The story is always different.

Dark matter particles floating in halos occasionally
collide and annihilate one another in tiny fireballs of radiation.

The fire next time.

Dr. Wefel and his colleagues have been chasing
sparks in the sky since 2000.

A wonderful job to have in this economy.

They spend the winter at McMurdo Station. Dr. Wefel
described it as very pleasant. "It's not bad until a storm
moves in. You put your hand out till you can't see it.
Then you go out and start shoveling snow."

It's starting to snow.

The data favored something even more exotic than supersymmetry,
namely a particle lost in the fifth dimension.

That's where my father's words go.

String theorists say there are at least six dimensions
beyond our simple grasp, wrapped up so tightly
we cannot see them or park in them.

Tightly, like my daughter's braids when she lets me make them
before bed. They're warm bread in the morning.
She unravels them—hair wavy down her back,
an imprint of last evening, a nod to what she said
as I was waking her for school—wait,
one more dream.

A particle in one of these dimensions
would not appear to us directly.

But maybe in a sky dream.

That theory was called "a delightful castle in the sky"
by Dr. Kane, who said he was glad
it kept Dr. Arkani-Hamed and his colleagues busy.

We are busy with him in the shadow light—the ordinary snow
melting on our tongues.

Father Reads Noah's Story from the Torah

This Saturday, his voice sounding the way
it must have when he was young and read
from the Williamsburg congregation's parchment,
his grandfather seated off to the side
checking the Hebrew pronunciations.
My father at 85 stands up strong

behind the *bima* and this time makes
no mistakes either. He knows the Five Books
of Moses by heart anyway, but still
he uses the silver *yad* to keep his place
as the animals go two by two into the ark
before the rain comes and lifts them high.

My father's voice catches when he reads
that God promises to never do this again.
At the service's end I wrap the Torah
with its belt, red velvet dress, gold trimming
and place it in its stand until it's time
for its return to the synagogue ark

facing east, so that when the sun rises
God remembers the covenant he made
after he smelled the sweet odor of burnt
blood rising from Noah's makeshift altar.
My father finds his seat next to me
in his *tallit* and looks out at the rain today.

Three Daughters

Once there was an old man
who had three daughters.
One married heaven, the second married fortune,
and the third—time.

On the right of his garden grew kindness,
the left knowledge,
and through the middle
a row of evil sprouted.

He built a fence around the plot,
leaving a place for love to break through.
It surprised him with fruit
that he had never tasted before.

Once there was an old man
who wanted to be young
so he drank from the night
and forgot his name.

He went fishing
and caught a carp
with two green eyes
and a violin between her fins.

Once there was an old man
who wouldn't take no for an answer.
He asked the world to be quiet
and there was silence.

He knocked on my door
and asked for light.
I gave him a cup
and he turned away.

Fireworks at Wilmington

The boom of revolution echoes—
      how it melts in our mouths,
            a whirring of having made it
                  to somewhere with no map, just you,

my love, here on the field, the night air

turns into yellow-eyed cats,
      and cotton candy, into a girl
            giggling and seventeen—
                  our bodies floating   out there.

A Continuum

The cart of sweets opens out over the boulevard
　　As if you could hear it—the man who takes your change
　　　Pauses for the sound of something other than the city
　　At 4:00 p.m. when the buildings are singed
　　　Gold and purple—the spires, water towers,
　　　　And clocks exhale and you do too.

Your mother and father sit at home by the fire this winter
　　Their movements, *limited,* she says.
　　Your son at 16—his whole body fills
　　His bed like the river
　　　With its slow moving ice, a visual
　　　For what is unstoppable,

A clear marker
　　A pitch forward to acceleration
　　A sign that these movements matter
　　In some universe
　　　Of ice and salt, sugar and cinnamon,
　　　Light and ligament.

At the Market

Radishes are pornographic—
      pink-red next to Ghandi, the Pork Flower Farm truck,
Bread Alone, and Fuck Bush Buttons—
      the man at the counter slices their heads off
for a dollar.

Strawberries, blueberries, tomatoes.
      Lemon thyme, currant scones, goat cheese on 14th street.
What is it about this that lifts us?
      Scallions, lavender, and McCouns.
My father's in a wheelchair now.
      And the four varieties of carrots, brown eggs, and cilantro.

Geraniums and moon flowers.
      I want to be a cluster of beets at noon,
lying open on the table, waiting to be
      sliced and served in a bowl
with garlic and parsley.

Pura Vida in Costa Rica

How does the light change red bricks,
smell of gasoline, cut grass,
gash below your heart?

When I was a child at the beach
I thought the day would never end
because it was how I had imagined it:

salt and blue, wind just right,
even the ice cream didn't melt.
Tell me what went wrong

between then and now.
I need to know for the next time
when I come back, and I'm lost

in shadow. Open the night shades,
yellow belt of daybreak wraps
around me and Elijah comes late,

the birds already singing
their new songs,
the monkeys flying from tree to tree

the way we might ask questions, trying
a conversation one way or another.
Their tails, an impetus for something

different, the two-toed sloth, too,
twenty hours a day, sleeping,
hugging her baby:

love in the tree
if only for me,
in the light of having seen it.

At 42

The cold enters the blue
day without snow.
I want the bush, berries,
dirt underneath
rich with worms.
Tell me something
about the topography of the soul.
I want chocolate
wrapped in silver,
love that sucks on you
like ten puppies until
all that's left is the dried teats
of having known it,
the milk and bread of us.
Where did that go?

Part IV:

Now She's in the World

Venice Fog

Sleep falls over him
as fog blankets Venice.

It eases over cathedrals.
Hidden doors. Muffled bells.

It lies over curving canals
and alleys, His new ribs

push and pull life
through him as he dreams.

The fog drifts away,
his eyelids slip back,

the highest domes
appearing in the distance.

He stirs. His hand flies up,
as the white pigeon

does at San Marco square.
Five fingers. I count again.

The Soft Spot

The soft spot grows smaller each day.
It beats like memory through his hair.

He gathers words for later.
When he needs them,

they will come falling out.
The diamond-shaped opening was kind.

It let his head mold and fit through me.
We spend our lives trying

to remember what we knew
before the earth closed tightly.

Fragment

When they began opening
the earth across the way
it was you I thought of.
You grew inside me, then stopped.

The workers dug into
the ground with drills and cranes.
They poured cement, started
to build upward.

At four o'clock the men went home.
It got quiet again.
I didn't drink enough milk.
"No," the radiologist said,

"It wasn't anything you did."
It was.
Life came for a moment—
then passed away.

The Watch

Early in the morning
as I rushed
to get dressed

I grabbed my watch.
It fell to the floor,
not shattering,

but opening.
The gold backing
fell to one side,

the glass cover
to the other.
The center piece

came into view
with all its tiny
cylindrical bits.

The hours came loose,
the minutes even
looser.

The seconds
dangled
there.

A moment flashed:
I wanted
to hold it

in my palm
but I snapped
it shut

and saw its faint line
of smoke disappear
into the daylight.

ew World

When you came out of me, I knew then
the earth was round.

I stare at you.
You look back at me with equal concern,

as if to say, "What will we do now
that we have found each other?"

Before the explorers came ashore
they must have taken a moment to rest,

as we do now together
your whole body fitting on my arm.

Pockets

When I am on my way, alone,
it's amusing to put my hand in my pocket
and find a pacifier or mitten,
but a discovery
to reach down and find a thought.

Once I pulled out
a note that read
"God touches with rain. The trees are his arms."
That's what my son said,
walking up First Avenue.

Three

When the moon is not full
my daughter asks who cut it.

She likes to touch my body,
wants to know what's behind the bones.

In her purple coat and red mittens
she walks with me to the park,

telling me about nursery school—
the snack and story of the day.

Now she's in the world,
like the tree on the hill,

wanting to sprout.

The Question

My six-year old asks me
if I had to choose

whether he or I should die,
who would I choose.

I say I would choose myself.
He asks again, surprised,

not believing me at first.
When he realizes I'm certain,

he walks off,
gets busy with something else.

I'm amazed at how
quickly I gave my life away,

as though my answer came
from an old story that's

been told over and over about
how we're made and made again.

ng

        ...y children are both screaming
ı run to comfort them,
one by holding close,
the other by talking and soothing.
I only have two arms.
I then wonder why so many hate their mothers.

I say to my mother and my mother's mother,
thank you for all that is here,
all that I know I will never know,
thank you for my tongue and teeth
so that I can taste the orange
and bite the brown bread.

The Crow

I want to taste the apple
on the edge of the field
where the fence begins. I sat
once for a long time until I could
make out the silhouette of the crow
and the night watchman.

Mother said,
No matter what you think boys are
stronger. You don't have a chance.
She meant it as a warning:
he'd be stronger.
Even the skinny ones.

48 Rue Lepic

I heard the bird toward morning,
the plane, and trucks, the neighbor
getting ready for work, making me
think of my father and what he'd say:

Your luck should be big.
What you need is your health.
A dumb old person is one
of the saddest things. Why?

Because he's gone through life
and hasn't learned anything.
At this hour water towers
are fierce.

A well in reverse
filled with dreams,
French and Yiddish words floating
through the pipes.

In Paris, we visited 48 Rue Lepic, where my parents lived in 1946.
My children stood in the doorway and I snapped photos, the street
curving to Sacre Coeur. We sat and waited during the sun shower
before climbing toward the church where the tourists were singing
and someone was playing the guitar, the music somehow wrapping
us all up so tightly.

The Night Riders

Zoe and Leora love the park at night.
Even though the gates are locked,

they slide through wide spaces
between the bars and sail

on their swings, standing up,
bare feet. Their nine-year old

bodies taut like rain. They fire
through the darkness almost

reaching the tops of sycamore
trees, then down again

only to rise once more
out of the blackness.

Part V:

The Little Room

i. Where the Stories Begin

Tiny lamps light you up in the corner.

You wear thin ties, gray pants
and listen like no one has ever listened.

It does not take long
for me to love you.

Your voice travels over the divide
to where the stories begin.

ii. The Clearing

When I saw him unzip
his elbow-patched sweater
and hang it in the closet
I wanted Mister Rogers to be my father.
Such evenness and predictability.

I craved his voice, the puppets,
the smallness of his show.
He spoke kindly to princes and princesses.

Before the end
the characters waved goodbye from a train
that wound through the kingdom.

Mister Rogers took off his slippers,
put his shoes back on
and led me home.

iii. Album

I show you old photographs.
Six chubby boys grin back at us, my older brothers.
Father is steady.
Mother has her arms around me.

Two inches from my face
That space between us softens.
You move back in your chair.
The session begins.

iv. The Stutter

Your stutter puts me at ease.
I want to cure you,
to loosen the words from your mouth
even before I speak.

One day you stop—like that,
as though I had oiled your mouth,
and let your words out.
Once yours loosened

mine came out too,
bigger and awkward at first
like new teeth pushing through the gum.
First I sat up and faced you.

Now I lie back
in your little room.
Words hang like banners.
It's all we have, just words.

v. Around Town

I see you all over the Upper West Side.

There are so many slight, bearded
middle-aged men, resembling Freud,
hurrying about, looking very busy.

When the purple plums are sticky
at the market, it's you on line
waiting to pay. Once I really do see
you in a cafe with another woman.

I get angry at the thought
that you aren't always in
the little room thinking of me.

vi. The Fight

You never say it
but I know you want
me to get angry.

So I do.
I leave before the session is over—
stomp out into the night.

I hope you stay
in the little room
until my hour is over.

The cool air feels good on my face.
I start to think how
it would be without you.

Part VI:

What I Was Then

The Tracks

On Saturday afternoons
we crossed the railroad tracks,
and light made diamonds on the Hudson River.

My mother held my hand
as we stepped high over
the third rail to safety

to where the bulrushes grew,
where the fishermen caught eels and smiled at us
as if we were another species.

I was seven.
I needed nothing
more than her.

Trains seldom passed.
When they did
the earth shook. The track did too,

but we remained upright,
not crossing back just then.
We stayed and waited

for quiet to settle along the river.
Tugboats moved slowly toward the ocean,
pulling time with their taut ropes.

Feeding the Elephants

Every Sunday morning after his office hours,
even in the rain,
my father took us to the zoo.

He drove my six brothers and me across the Bronx
with old bread in the back seat
given by his patient, a baker.

Lions slept late on Sundays,
all looking like Bach.
Their ears twitched occasionally.

The keeper threw black fish to seals.
Seals flew, landing in the water,
only to chew and rise again.

Father carried the bag of bread
around the corner.
The elephants were waiting for him.

He pulled round corn bread from the bag,
hurled it over the stone wall.
The male came forward,

and with his trunk he smacked the bread
against cement until it broke.
Piece by piece he put into his mouth.

Father laughed until the tears came.
When he caught his breath,
he threw rye breads over. The females liked those.

When we were sure that everyone was fed
father called it a day
and led us home.

Separate Seating

In the synagogue
where my brothers sat with my father,
I sat alone,
wedged between old women.

The rabbi placed the ram's horn
between his lips and blew
first short, then longer sounds
ending with a cry long enough

for Sarah, Rebecca, Leah, and Rachel
to come through the window
and sit by my side.

They smelled like the desert.
Their necklaces glittered.
They poured me warm sweet water
from a clay jug.

Before the rabbi had taken the shofar from his mouth
they left with their jewels and urns,
leaving me sand
between the pages of my prayer book.

Winter Garlic, 1979

I wondered
how my father could
move under all that wool
when he took his evening run
and layered his body
in sweaters, wrapping a handmade one
around his waist for good luck.

He outlined
the route before leaving
the house, as if planning
a military maneuver,
uncertain of its success.

Back at home
he undressed in front of
the three-way mirror
until he could see his bare chest,
strong like an old tree trunk,
its roots still cracking pavement.

Then he drank,
breathing slowly and watching
his ribs make waves as if his breath
was pulled by the moon.
He smelled of sweat and beer.

In other itchy
knits he entered
the kitchen and sat
by the cutting board table
below the radio.
A cast iron pot of beef
waited for him. Raw garlic, too.

Before the Israeli
news began over WEVD,
he told me how cold
it was on the bridge
and offered me garlic.
We talked until *Bruchim Haba'im*
rang clear across the counter.

When I slice
cloves on my own board,
removing their silky
coats before cutting through,
I smell my father
his skin stretched tight, papery.

Her Boutique

At the Salvation Army
she looked for the past,
before the war.

"You can't find things anywhere else
like you can here,"
My mother would say when I wanted new things.

She touched chipped china with cherry designs,
cotton blouses, jeans with broken zippers
in the room as large as a bowling alley.

The rows of clothing had little
regard for order.
Socks scattered like refugees.

When we were done
the beautiful black woman with big-hooped earrings
would put our items in paper bags,

wrapping the chosen shirts and pants
around the dishes that mother
would now call her own.

Sunnies

When I was eight and David Linley was ten,
we'd go to Vernmoore Pond with our poles,
red and white bobbers, nets, and pail of worms.
We'd drive a worm through a hook, arch

our rods way back, then pitch forward.
The line would sail, land, and settle.
We'd lie on our stomachs and wait
for a ripple for the bobber to go under.

Then we'd rise and reel it in, not knowing
what was pulling until the fish rose out
of the water: a small orange-bellied
sunny, cold and silvery, sharp fins.

I'd put my hand around it, hold it firm,
undo the hook from its green mouth,
throw it back in. Watch it swim
into our shadows, away from us.

Making Jam

My mother and I picked ripe gooseberries
from bushes next to the hole
where we threw eggshells.
"That makes the best dirt,"
she would say and point
to the worms moving through the earth.

I cut the stems with scissors.
She used a pocket knife.
Together we sat on the steps
and touched each green berry before
dropping it into the pot.

Putting it on the stove,
she added water and sugar.
I stirred with a wooden spoon.
Hours later I lifted the lid.
Everything was sweet.

The berries burst.
Their skins and seeds formed a mass
of red she said was God-given.
We shouldn't waste any.
We filled every jar in the house with it,
jars that once held other things.

Every Friday after sundown,
my mother, cousin Heddy, and I
would go to old movies at the library.
Black and white. Katherine Hepburn and Ingrid Bergman.

We'd sit in a row, riveted. Heddy, her white hair
tended to, the way she would her garden.
She was big boned in that grand style.
If we just tapped the screen we too could crawl

into the *African Queen.* After the movie
we walked to the car, and my mother would
ask Heddy if she liked it. *It was a good one,*
she'd say. Then we'd drive her home,

watch as she'd walk into the night,
up her front steps, reaching into her pocket
for keys. For a moment, she was a star
who got kissed, fading as we pulled away.

My Father and Jackson Pollock

Before I was born my parents
were friends with Jackson and Lee
when they were neighbors in the Springs.

My father wrestled and joked with Jackson.
He liked to come over
and horse around with my brothers.

Looking at his paintings in the museum,
I thought this is what I was then—
Lavender Mist, *Yellow Islands*, *White Light*.

Last summer I went to the tip of Long Island
to see his studio and our old house.
They were both bolted shut.
But the grounds were open.

I saw the view of the marsh,
the openness,
felt the thin long grass
that sways with a whisper.

My father watched Jackson paint.
He once asked him what he was doing.
Jackson said he was painting what he saw.

My father remembers the call when Jackson died.
One time he'd offered my father a painting.
"Take any of that crap." he told him.

Antibes in Spring

Even a bicycle
leaning by a gate
makes you stop.
A clothesline between two buildings
hung with some woman's stockings, dresses,
were draped just so, for you.

Picasso dipped his brush
into this light, which now
strokes the dove on your terrace.
It coos and flies off
into the cool afternoon
when the sun begins
falling into the bluest sea.

Father Turns 80

My father said he once saw Eleanor Roosevelt
wearing a big hat
hurrying along 42nd Street.

He also saw Winston Churchill getting out of a cab.
He said his eyes were so blue,
blue like he never had seen.

He also talked about his Paris days,
when he was a student at the Sorbonne after the war,
and how they loved Americans, especially him.

Father said these things one Sunday afternoon.
I looked at him and wondered
what will my children believe were my moments

stretching out behind them?
What will they hold up and say,
"That was my mother's time?"

Notes

Barbara Staudacher and Heinz Högerle provided me with the archives of my mother's family's history in Rexingen, Germany, and showed me the places that inspired many of the poems in Part II. They provided me with the photo of the original envelope that contained one of my grandfather's letters. The photo appears on the cover.

Audrey Pfeil translated my grandfather's original letters from German that appear in "Two Letters." Belinda Cooper translated additional documents about my grandfather that were part of an exhibit in Rexingen on Jewish soldiers that fought for the Germans in World War I.

In "Moss," the word *"Glühwein"* means mulled wine in German.

An excerpt from Friedrich Schiller's "Ode to Joy" appears in "Above the Stars."

In "Cemetery in Basingen (town neighboring Rexingen)" "Cohanim" are Jewish High Priests. The poem refers to the symbol showing two hands arranged for the priestly blessing, which identifies a Cohan and appears on tombstones.

Some of the language in "Wait, One More Dream" was taken from a November 25, 2008 *New York Times* article "A Whisper, Perhaps, From the Universe's Dark Side," by Dennis Overbye.

In "Father Reads Noah's Story from the Torah," the meanings of the Hebrew words are as follows: "Bima" is a raised platform from which the Torah is read. "Yad" is a pointer tapering into the shape of a closed hand with an extended index finger used as a guide for the Torah reader. "Tallit" is a prayer shawl worn over the head or shoulders.

In "Winter Garlic, 1979," the Hebrew words "Bruchim Haba'im" mean welcome.

About the Author

Sarah Stern is the author of *But Today Is Different* (Wipf and Stock) and *Another Word for Love* (Finishing Line Press). She is a five-time winner of the Bronx Council on the Arts' BRIO Poetry Award. She graduated from Barnard College and Columbia University's Graduate School of Journalism. You can see more of her work at www.sarahstern.me.